Kids Connecting to Christ
COLORING BOOK

By Maurice M. Jenkins

Disclaimer
Copyrights Reserved© 2023

No part of this eBook can be transmitted or reproduced in any form, including print, electronic, photocopying, scanning, mechanical, or recording, without prior written permission from the author.

★ ★ ★ ★ ★ ★ ★ ★ ★ ★ ★ ★

The Birth of Jesus Christ

In Bethlehem, a young woman named Mary gave birth to a son, through the power of the Holy Spirit, whom she named Jesus. Mary and her husband Joseph had to place to stay so they settled in a stable where horses and goats lived. The baby did not have a crib to sleep in, but was laid in a manger. During this time an angel appeared to some shephards near Bethlehem, who were attending to their flock. The angel gave them the good news about the birth of Jesus Christ and told them that they could find him sleeping in a manger. The shepherds left their flock to go and find baby Jesus.

By Maurice M. Jenkins

* * * * * * * * * * *

Jesus in the Temple

When Jesus was 12 years old, his family went to Jerusalem to celebrate the Passover festival. After the festival came to an end, Mary and Joseph left to return home, but Jesus stayed behind in the temple. His parents were worried and searched for him for three days, until they found him in the temple, talking to the teachers and asking them questions. Jesus was learning in the temple with the elders and the priests for three days. Not only was he learning from the teachers he also asked questions which amazed the high priests who were present in the temple.

The Baptism of Jesus

Jesus came to John the Baptist while he was baptizing other people in the river. John tried to make Jesus change his mind, but Jesus answered, "In this way we will do all that God requires." So, John agreed to baptize Jesus. Jesus was baptized by John the Baptist in the Jordan River. When he came up out of the water, the heavens opened and a voice from heaven said, "This is my Son, whom I love; with him I am well pleased." After his baptism, Jesus began his ministry, traveling throughout Galilee and preaching the gospel of the kingdom of God.

By Maurice M. Jenkins

★ ★ ★ ★ ★ ★ ★ ★ ★ ★ ★

Jesus Blesses the Children

One day, Jesus was teaching a large crowd of people when some parents brought their children to him, hoping that he would bless them. But the disciples tried to shoo the children away, thinking that they were a nuisance. Jesus saw what was happening and said, "Let the little children come to me, and do not hinder them, for the kingdom of heaven belongs to such as these." He then blessed the children and held them in his arms, showing that he valued and loved them just as much as the adults. Jesus is clear in his teachings that children are an important part of the kingdom of God. Jesus also teaches us that the kingdom of heaven belongs to those who are like these children.

✵ ✵ ✵ ✵ ✵ ✵ ✵ ✵ ✵ ✵ ✵

The Boy with the Loaves and Fishes

Jesus was teaching a large crowd of people, but they were hungry and didn't have any food. A young boy approached Jesus and offered him his lunch, which consisted of five loaves of bread and two fish. Andrew, Simon Peter's brother said, "here is a boy with five loaves of bread and two fish, but that is not enough for so many people." Jesus took the boy's loaves of bread and two fishand gave thanks to God, then miraculously multiplied the food so that everyone in the crowd had enough to eat. The boy's small act of generosity had a huge impact, showing that even a little can go a long way.

By Maurice M. Jenkins

★ ★ ★ ★ ★ ★ ★ ★ ★ ★ ★ ★

The Lost Sheep

Jesus once told a story about a shepherd who had 100 sheep, but one of them went missing. The shepherd left the other 99 sheep and went to search for the lost one, determined to find it. When he finally found the lost sheep, he rejoiced and celebrated, saying, "*I tell you that in the same way, there will be more rejoicing in heaven over one sinner who repents than over ninety-nine righteous persons who do not need to repent.*" This story shows that every person, even the smallest and weakest among us, is important and valued in God's eyes.

By Maureen M. Jenkins

The Samaritan Woman's Daughter

A woman from Samaria approached Jesus, asking him to heal her daughter who was possessed by a demon. Jesus spoke to the woman and said, "Woman, great is your faith. Let it be done for you as you wish." The woman's daughter was instantly healed, showing that even a mother's faith can bring about miraculous results.

By Maurice M. Jenkins

* * * * * * * * * * * *

Jesus once said, "*Truly I tell you, unless you change and become like little children, you will never enter the kingdom of heaven.*" This statement emphasizes the importance of childlike faith, humility, and simplicity in our relationship with God. Children have a natural innocence and purity that we can learn from, and Jesus encourages us to approach God with the same trust and openness that children exhibit.

★ ★ ★ ★ ★ ★ ★ ★ ★ ★ ★ ★

Walking on Water

When Jesus noticed the disciples struggling against the fierce wind he walked out to them on water.When His followers first saw Him, they mistook Him for a ghost and shouted out in terror. He soothed them, and Peter asked if he, too, could walk on water. Jesus responded yes, as long as he focused on Him.When Peter stepped out of the boat he began to sink. Jesus saved Peter, and asked, "*Why did you doubt*?" The moral of this story is focus on Jesus and do not doubt.

★ ★ ★ ★ ★ ★ ★ ★ ★ ★ ★ ★

The Lost Sheep

Most of the Pharisees had a problem with Jesus because He ate with the sinners and allowed them to follow Him. Jesus told them this parable to help them understand. "If one of you has 100 sheep and even if one is lost, will you not leave the rest and go to look for the lost sheep? When you find it, you are very happy and tell everyone that you found your lost sheep. You will call your friends and celebrate. In the same way, when a sinner repents, there is a lot of rejoicing in heaven."

★ ★ ★ ★ ★ ★ ★ ★ ★ ★ ★

The Three Wise Men

At the time Jesus's birth, there were three wise men, called the magi, who saw a brilliant star in the distance. They followed the star to find the new king. When the three wise men found the baby in the manger they knelt and prayed and gave him gifts of gold and myrrh. Then they travelled home on a different path from where they came to avoid being caught by king Herod, who was the king of Judah and wanted to kill the baby.

★ ★ ★ ★ ★ ★ ★ ★ ★ ★ ★ ★

The Healing of the Blind Man

When Jesus arrived at the village of Bethsaida, which is in Galilee, he was asked to heal a blind man. Jesus took the man by the hand and led him outside of village. Jesus Christ cured the blind man's eyesight by simply touching his eyes. Jesus asked him, "Do you see?" and the man said, "I see men, but they look like trees, walking." This story teaches us the power of faith and the importance of seeking healing from the one who can truly provide it.

★ ★ ★ ★ ★ ★ ★ ★ ★ ★ ★

The Sermon on the Mount

Jesus Christ delivered one of his most famous sermons, where he spoke about love, mercy, and forgiveness. This story shows us the importance of treating others with kindness and compassion. This is the time when Jesus thought his disciples the Lord's Prayer and also shared with them several parables. The Sermon on the Mount is an important event for us all because it is where Jesus talked about the Beatitudes and various other teachings about God's laws which are expected to be upheld by everyone of us.

* * * * * * * * * * * *

The Woman at the Well

Jesus Christ spoke with a Samaritan woman at a well, offering her water that would quench her thirst forever. This story reminds us that God's love is available to everyone, regardless of their background. The story of the woman brings our attention to the central theme of the Gospel. In this story, Jesus demonstrates his care for every human being, regardless of their social standing. In the end, her continuing witness to Jesus, brought many towards the Christian faith, and she was eventually described as "equal to the

By Maurice M. Jenkins

The Transfiguration

Jesus Christ revealed his divine nature to his disciples by transfiguring before them, shining with a heavenly light. This story shows us the power and majesty of God. The story of the transfiguration reminds us all that regardless of how powerful a spiritual experience may be, the time comes when we all must come down from the mountain and return to our everyday lives. But, when we do return, we must do so as a changed person. It is also a reminder that there is a divine hand which is always at work in the events of our lives.

By Maurice M. Jenkins

★ ★ ★ ★ ★ ★ ★ ★ ★ ★ ★ ★

The Parable of the Good Samaritan

Jesus Christ taught about loving our neighbors by sharing the story of a Samaritan who showed kindness to a stranger in need. This story teaches us the importance of being compassionate and helping those around us.

★ ★ ★ ★ ★ ★ ★ ★ ★ ★ ★

The Healing of the Centurion's Servant

While Jesus was travelling, a centurion heard of his arrival and sent some elders to greet Jesus. During that time, Jesus was asked to heal a servant of the centurion. They pleaded in earnest saying, this man deserves to be healed because he loves our nation and has built many synagogues, so Jesus went with them and said, "I tell you, not even in Israel have I found such faith." Jesus Christ healed a servant of a Roman centurion, showing that his love and mercy extends to all people, regardless of their nationality or social status.

By Maurice M. Jenkins

★ ★ ★ ★ ★ ★ ★ ★ ★ ★ ★ ★

The Resurrection of Lazarus

Jesus Christ raised his friend Lazarus from the dead, showing his power over death and the promise of eternal life for all who believe in him. The raising of Lazarus teaches us an important lesson, which is that even when we feel God is doing nothing, He is doing more than we could ever imagine. While Lazarus was entombed for four days when Jesus arrived in the town of Bethany, he was still raised from the dead at Jesus' command and emerged alive from inside the tomb in his burial clothing.

By Maurice M. Jenkins

★ ★ ★ ★ ★ ★ ★ ★ ★ ★ ★

The Cleansing of the Temple

Jesus Christ drove out the money changers from the temple, showing his passion for true worship and devotion to God. What we learn from this is that it takes great work, effort and patience, but we all must have faith that He will give us all that has been promised in the end, no matter what difficulties we are faced with today.

By Maurice M. Jenkins

★ ★ ★ ★ ★ ★ ★ ★ ★ ★ ★

The Healing of the Leper

Jesus Christ cured a leper's disease by touching him, showing his compassion for those who are outcast and rejected by society. As the leper kneels before him, Jesus blesses him. Rather than warning Jesus of his ailment, the leper makes a statement of his faith and begs Jesus to heal him. Jesus answers the leper, saying that he will heal him, and the man is miraculously healed. The leper knew the Jesus has the power to heal him of his ailment and as soon as Jesus had spoken the leper was healed.

★ ★ ★ ★ ★ ★ ★ ★ ★ ★ ★ ★

The Sermon on the Plain

Jesus Christ gave another powerful sermon, where he taught about humility, forgiveness, and the importance of living a life centered on God. Jesus delivered this sermon on the plain after he came down from the mountain. Jesus gave the sermon on the plain while standing at a level place and addressing an audience that came from nearby towns and villages. During the sermon on the plain, Jesus gives several commands, including; love your enemies, do good onto those who hate you, bless those who curse you and pray for all those who are spiteful towards you. The sermon on the plain is where Jesus gave a well-known commandment, "Do onto others as you would have them do to you."

By Maurice M. Jenkins

* * * * * * * * * * *

The Parable of the Mustard Seed

Jesus Christ compared the kingdom of God to a tiny mustard seed, showing us the power of faith and the impact it can have on our lives and the world around us. The mustard seed is considered to be the smallest of seeds, and yet, it grew ito a huge plant. Jesus Christ teaches us that while the kingdom of God began small, with Jesus, it would grow and spread throughout the world. This parable is followed by the parable of the leaven which also shares the same theme that the Kingdom of Heaven grew from small beginnings.

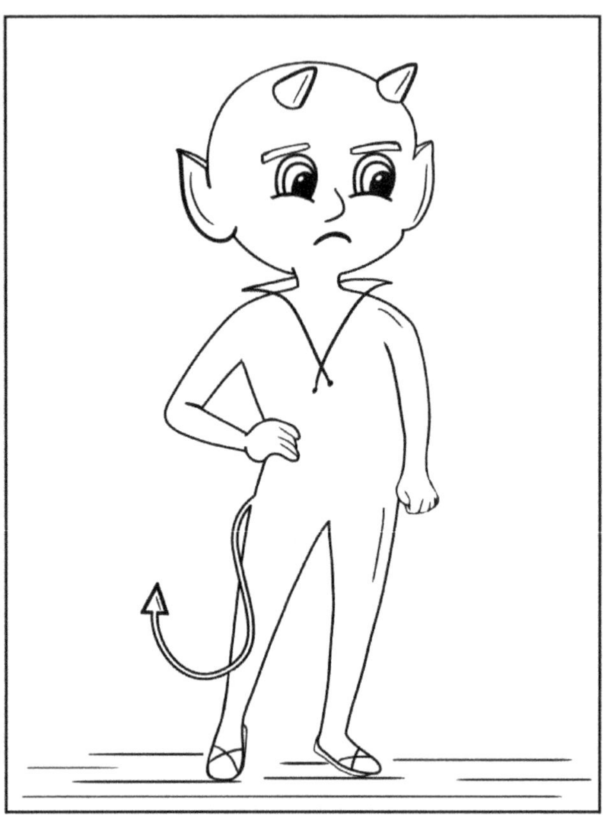

★ ★ ★ ★ ★ ★ ★ ★ ★ ★ ★

The Healing of the Demon-Possessed Man

Jesus Christ freed a man from a legion of demons, showing his power over evil and the hope he offers for those who are oppressed. The power of Jesus can be seen in his ability to not only cast out the powers of darkness, but also converse with them who we humans cannot see. With the power of God, Jesus commands the demons to go into a herd of pigs that are nearby and the demons obey. The herd of pigs then jump into the sea and drown. The men who were attending to the pigs were left stunned and confused, and at once rushed into town to tell the others what they had witnessed.

By Maurice M. Jenkins

★ ★ ★ ★ ★ ★ ★ ★ ★ ★ ★

The Parable of the Sower

Jesus Christ shared a parable about a sower who scattered seeds, showing us the importance of cultivating our hearts and minds to receive the message of God's love. This parable is an allegory of the kingdom of God. We learn that the human heart is like a soil that is receptive to the seed of the Word of God. The soil which the seed falls on represents the four conditions of the heart; the fruitful heart, the crowded heart, the shallow heart and the hard heart. The good news is that we are the ones who determine what kind of soil represents our hearts. This is why Jesus said, "Lay aside all filthiness and overflow of wickedness and receive with meekness the implanted Word which saves souls."

✦ ✦ ✦ ✦ ✦ ✦ ✦ ✦ ✦ ✦ ✦

Jesus Christ shared a final meal with his disciples, where he broke bread and drank wine to symbolize his sacrifice for our sins. This story reminds us of the power of the sacraments and the importance of living a life of service and sacrifice. In this story, we are reminded of the importance of living and working for Jesus. It is also an anticipation of the glorious feast which awaits us on the final day of judgement. The Last Supper serves as just a taste of what is to come, which will be true life.

By Maurice M. Jenkins

★ ★ ★ ★ ★ ★ ★ ★ ★ ★ ★ ★

The Blessing of the Children

Jesus Christ welcomed children into his arms, blessed them, and said, "Let the little children come to me, and do not hinder them, for the kingdom of God belongs to such as these." This story reminds us of the value and importance of children in the eyes of God.

★ ★ ★ ★ ★ ★ ★ ★ ★ ★ ★ ★

Jesus Christ is the Way, the Truth, and the Life

Jesus Christ teaches us that the entrance to heaven is a small gate and narrow is its path that leads to the Kingdom of God. There is absolutely no other way to enter the kingdom of God and have eternal life. Jesus warns us all to stay away from the wide gate that promises a full life because ultimately, it leads us away from God and the eternal life that we shall have in heaven.

By Maurice M. Jenkins

★ ★ ★ ★ ★ ★ ★ ★ ★ ★ ★ ★

The Rebuke of the Disciples:

Jesus Christ rebuked his disciples for trying to keep children away from him, saying, "Let the little children come to me, and do not hinder them, for the kingdom of heaven belongs to such as these." This story shows us the value of children in the eyes of God and the importance of including them in our communities and worship.

✶ ✶ ✶ ✶ ✶ ✶ ✶ ✶ ✶ ✶ ✶

The Healing of the Sick Children

Jesus Christ healed many sick children who were brought to him, showing his love and care for the most vulnerable in society. During the three years of Jesus' ministry he met with the parents of many children whom he had cured and also raised from the dead. In each of these stories, there is a special message for us all. Unfortunately, sickness and pain are all around us. So, let's put our trust in God and remember that He loves us and that he wants the very best for us, even when we are sick.

By Maurice M. Jenkins

★ ★ ★ ★ ★ ★ ★ ★ ★ ★ ★ ★

The parable of the lost sheep is one of the parables of Jesus. Jesus Christ shared the story of a shepherd who left his flock to search for a lost sheep, showing us the depth of God's love and his desire to save all who are lost, including children. The parable tells us about the beautiful meaning of God who seeks out all who are lost, even the sinners and rejoices when they are found. This is because God cares and loves us all equally, because we serev a Good Shepherd. In the same way, we have been called on to love and care for all those who are lost.

★ ★ ★ ★ ★ ★ ★ ★ ★ ★ ★ ★

The Curing of the Epileptic Child

Jesus Christ cured an epileptic child, showing his power over sickness and disease and his desire to bring healing to all, including children. This is a wonderful story about restoration and healing. The little boy is brough to Jesus and experiences the love of Jesus and is miraculously healed.

* * * * * * * * * * *

The Story of Mary and Martha

Jesus Christ praised Mary for sitting at his feet and learning from him, showing us the importance of valuing and investing in the spiritual growth of children. The story of Mary and Martha teaches us all that we need to be more like them. We also need to keep all of our priorities in the right order. Regardless of how busy our lives may get, we need to always seek out God and put Him first above all things in everthing we do.

The Parable of the Good Samaritan

Jesus Christ taught about loving our neighbors by sharing the story of a Samaritan who showed kindness to a stranger in need. This story teaches us the importance of being compassionate and helping children in need. When the Samaritan saw the man who was injured and lying by the roadside, he took pity on him and bandaged his wounds. He then took him to the innkeeper who he paid to look after him. This parable ends with Jesus commanding us to go out and do the same as the Samaritan did.

By Maurice M. Jenkins

The Resurrection of the Daughter of Jairus

Jesus Christ raised the daughter of Jairus from the dead, showing his power over death and his promise of eternal life for all who believe in him, including children. The raising of Jairus' daughter is a miracle of Jesus that occurs and is interwoven with the account of the healing of a bleeding woman. The story of Jairus' daughter teaches us about the miraculous faith through suffering. Jesus healed Jairus' daughter by taking her hand and saying, "Little girl, get up." It was because of Jairus' faith that Jesus was able to heal his daughter.

By Maurice M. Jenkins

★ ★ ★ ★ ★ ★ ★ ★ ★ ★ ★ ★

The Parable of the Prodigal Son

In this parable, a son demands his inheritance from his father and leaves to live a life of debauchery. He eventually realizes his mistakes and returns to his father, who forgives him with open arms. This story teaches us about the power of unconditional forgiveness and love. This parable teaches us that sin is always against God. But repentance opens the way to God's forgiveness. The parable of the prodigal son is considered to be one of the greatest stories of redemption ever told because it is a story that is filled with grace and mercy. It also teaches us that God loves us all equally and that we can repent and turn to God at any time.

★ ★ ★ ★ ★ ★ ★ ★ ★ ★ ★ ★

The Forgiveness of Peter

When Jeuss was washing his disciple's feet, Peter said, "No! you shall enver wash my feet." Then Jesus said to him, "Unless I wash you, you have no part with me." After denying Jesus three times, Peter is forgiven and reinstated by Jesus. This story teaches us about the power of forgiveness and how even the most serious of sins can be forgiven if we are truly sorry and repentant.

The Day of Pentecost

The Holy Spirit descends upon the disciples, enabling them to speak in different languages and proclaim the gospel to people from all over the world. This story marks the beginning of the church's mission to share the good news of Jesus Christ with all people. The Day of Pentecost commemorates the descent of the Holy Spirit on the Apostles and follows the crucifixion, resurrection and ascension of Jesus Christ. This day also marks the beginning of the mission of the Christian Church in the world.

✱ ✱ ✱ ✱ ✱ ✱ ✱ ✱ ✱ ✱ ✱ ✱

The Forgiveness of the Debtors

In this parable, a king forgives the debts of his servants. One servant, who was forgiven a large debt, refuses to forgive a smaller debt owed to him by another servant. The king punishes the unmerciful servant for his lack of forgiveness. This story teaches us about the importance of forgiving others, as we have been forgiven ourselves.

Author's Name: Maurice M Jenkins

mauricej50.com

mmj660149@yahoo.com

www.ingramcontent.com/pod-product-compliance
Lightning Source LLC
Chambersburg PA
CBHW050621160726

48003CB00003B/1284